MONKS ROAD

MONKS ROAD

Gethsemani into the Twenty-First Century

From Desert to Cloister
By Michael Casey, OCSO

From the Old World to the New
By Clyde F. Crews

FROM DESERT TO CLOISTER

By Michael Casey, OCSO

F OR MORE THAN A CENTURY AND A HALF the Abbey of Gethsemani has been home to a community of Cistercian monks following a simple life of prayer and work while living somewhat apart from the cares and concerns of the rest of the world. Visitors to the monastery experience it not only as a quiet place of peace but also as a center of warm and friendly hospitality where all are accepted as they are and are welcomed in the name of Christ. After visiting, people often wish to know more about how the monastery came to be, what is its history, and what motivates the men who come to spend their lives here.

Gethsemani is part of an international network that includes 178 monasteries in forty-five countries. In the United States alone there are twelve monasteries of monks and five of nuns. The Cistercian Order has, for nearly a thousand years, provided a structure and support for men and women who wish to dedicate their lives to God by following the Gospel path described in the Rule of Saint Benedict. Today, more than 3,500 monks and nuns wear the same habit, follow the same way of life, share a common history, and are inspired by the same spirituality.

The best way to understand this way of life is to see how it has evolved through the centuries. The values that continue to motivate those who embrace the monastic life developed slowly, often triggered by particular circumstances. Hence, monastic history is not

Saint Benedict

480–547

simply the external story of how the monastic institution developed; it is also an account of how its characteristic beliefs and values arose to meet the challenges of the times.

THE CALL

On the margins of many cultures we often find individuals and groups who move away from common social concerns to dedicate themselves to cultivating their relationship with the invisible world of the spirit. This withdrawal from ordinary life is not so much motivated by disgust at the way most people live or by a desire to escape from it. Rather, it has its origin in some intangible experience of inner enlightenment, in which material urgencies fade away for a time, and the unseen reality of the spiritual world begins to be perceived. This moment marks the dawn of a spiritual sense which henceforth will clamor silently for attention, threatening to unseat the certainties by which a person's life has hitherto been governed. The work of conversion begins when someone is seized by a formless attraction to a transcendent reality. The person is called, as Abraham was called, to go forth from a familiar land and to journey with the unseen God toward a more abundant life. Because of this experience, a person is drawn to a greater interest in spiritual reality and so begins a slow process of disengagement from secular affairs.

Those who are called feel as though they have been somehow touched by God. They do not fully understand what is happening, and they themselves are not understood by those around them. The mystery of the divine presence has made an uninvited intrusion into their lives, and they are bewildered and, perhaps, a little fearful. For some people the experience is dramatic and its effect is instantaneous and overwhelming. Think of the conversion of Saint Paul on the road to Damascus. For others, the process drags on naggingly in the back-

ground for an extended period. Saint Augustine argued and struggled for seventeen long years against the grace that had been given him. Like him, many who feel the touch of God's hand upon them will experience simultaneously a warm attraction to follow its lead and a stubborn determination to leave their lives unchanged. And a few unhappy people will choose to ignore the moment and to build a wall of denial around it to insulate their lives from its influence.

The work of conversion begins when someone is seized by a formless attraction to a transcendent reality.

Every person who is conscious of this call experiences it in a different way. For some, it is a subtle interior stirring, like a soft breeze on the surface of the soul. In others, an attraction to an alternative life comes through the example of persons in whom the light of holiness shines. Or it may be a word spoken by a wise mentor or read in a book that changes the direction of their thinking and acting. In some, God intervenes in a time of crisis, when their former life is in ruins and the future seems bleak. Just as one door closes, another seems to open before them and they are drawn to pass through it.

The monks dedicate themselves to the worship of God in a hidden life within the monastery under the Rule of St. Benedict. They lead a monastic way of life in solitude and silence, in assiduous prayer and joyful penitence, thus rendering to the divine majesty a service that is at once humble and noble.

From the Order's Constitutions

The most common reaction to this experience is wonderment.
Like Moses at the burning bush, there is a tendency to turn aside in
order to look more closely into this unforeseen happening. Different people respond differently. Some seek solitude so that they may
ponder within themselves the meaning of what has transpired. Some
seek the counsel of an experienced elder who can explain to them
the significance of what they have experienced. And nearly everyone
looks for the support of a group of people who have passed through a
similar experience, in the hope that the flickering flame may not be
extinguished through ignorance or neglect.

The monastic impulse derives its energy from this experience of
being called by God. Monasticism is not a job to be done, as it were,
a vacant position awaiting a newcomer to occupy it. Being drawn
to monasticism is entirely a response to a life-changing movement
coming from deep within the individual, one that initiates a lifelong
desire for a closer and more intense relationship with God. It is more
a matter of the heart than of the head.

FOLLOWING CHRIST

The central component of a vocation to monastic life is this mysterious
attraction to spirituality that translates itself into an active seeking of
God. The experience is supported by a willingness to devote a substantial part of one's energies in responding to the call. It is this practical
determination to leave behind everything in order to follow Christ
that signals that spiritual desire comes from deep inside a person and
is not merely a superficial interest in the monastic lifestyle and culture. Nor is it some form of pious daydreaming that will lead nowhere.
The kingdom of heaven is like treasure hidden under the soil; to take
possession of that treasure it is necessary to sell everything and acquire
the land in which the treasure lies. The double imperative of letting go
and laying hold of something sets up a rhythm that will last a lifetime.

A typical response to the grace of conversion is to enact a radical
change in lifestyle. We see this in the narratives of the Acts of the
Apostles. The first believers came together to experience solidarity
and communion in their newfound faith, living together, breaking
bread and praying together, sharing their goods, and being "one in

Different people respond differently. Some seek solitude so that they may ponder within themselves the meaning of what has transpired.

heart and mind." Later generations would look back with nostalgia on this seemingly idyllic period, even though the early Church also had its share of infidelities and conflicts.

In the generations following the time of the apostles the experience of persecution by the state and the prospect of martyrdom helped believers to develop a better sense of identity as Christians separated by faith and practice from their fellow citizens. In time, clusters of Christians came to live together in more or less organized groups to support one another in living the gospels more intensely and permanently. Experienced leaders emerged from within these groups who were able to guide and animate those who came, teaching them how to live a more disciplined life and to escape the temptations that await any who choose to pursue the spiritual path.

The more these early practitioners strove to live in accordance with the gospels, the more they found themselves set apart from the world around them, from its official religion, and from its pagan rites and celebrations. To avoid compromising their beliefs and values, Christians were obliged to reduce their active participation in public affairs and live as fringe-dwellers. The more committed among them strove to create their own environment in which they would be free to live holy lives without having to contend with unsympathetic surroundings.

The sisters of the monastery of Tautra, Norway, at prayer in choir. Opposite: Meditation in the abbey church at Gethsemani.

SOLITUDE

Remembering the example of Jesus, whose practice it was to withdraw to deserted places in order to have space for prayer, the most fervent began to seek a place of quiet in the deserts of Egypt and Palestine, leaving behind family, career, and possessions in order to live for God alone. The most famous of these was Saint Antony of Egypt, who was a monk for more than seventy years, resisting a variety of temptations, being drawn into deep prayer, attracting a crowd of followers and disciples, and instructing them in the ways of Gospel living.

As a result, Saint Athanasius tells us in his *Life of Antony* that the Egyptian desert had become like a city, so populous had the arrival of so many new monks made it. Although, for practical reasons, some monks clustered together to form little monastic colonies, most pursued an individual lifestyle, living a life of poverty and prayer according to their own lights. At about the same time that Antony was moving into deeper solitude, Pachomius was organizing large communities of monks organized like a military camp, but this was not the predominant shape of monasticism at that time. Apart from coming together to participate in the Eucharist on Sundays, most monks lived separately; they kept to their tiny cells, working quietly to support themselves and trying to become more attuned to the divine presence that somehow seemed closer the farther they were from the city.

These monks in their great variety were like Abraham. They heard the divine voice calling them to go forth from their native land and from their families, and, like Abraham, they lived in the hope of coming into possession of a promised land—the heavenly homeland to which they so fervently aspired. Living at a distance from family and friends, from secular society, from ambitions and possessions, becomes a defining feature of monastic life.

SPIRITUAL WARFARE

Men and women of all ages and from different levels of society thronged the desert—so it was said—seeking solitude and silence and aspiring to a state of continual prayer. But once they had located an isolated place in which to settle, a new challenge appeared. Their bodies were stable enough, but their thoughts compensated by

In the fields around the Abbey of Bamenda, Cameroon.

Saint Antony

251–356

Saint Pachomius

292–346

becoming highly mobile. Wild fantasies began to rampage through their imagination, reminding them of their family and friends, conjuring up all the activities they had so recently renounced, evoking all the pleasures of a comfortable life, disturbing their tranquility, and drawing their hearts away from the single goal they had proposed for themselves.

Just as Jesus himself experienced, the desert was a place of ongoing temptation. Even while these newly hatched monks tried to design for themselves a lifestyle that corresponded with their spiritual aspirations, they found that their outward good works were often accompanied by an interior clamor of alternative images, suggestions, and desires. The prospect of a quiet life that had drawn them into the desert began to seem illusory, and thoughts of returning to their former way of life—or, worse still, of abandoning their spiritual quest—troubled and wearied them. Worst of all was the insistent gnawing of self-reproach and guilt because the temptations seemed to come from deep inside them.

In desperation these troubled monks sought counsel from those more experienced than themselves. They treasured the advice they received and remembered it, sharing it with others in similar situations. And so a body of teaching was generated, later collected as *The Sayings of the Desert Fathers*. Tradition has passed on to us several series of such sayings, all marked by common sense, psychological insight, a radical commitment to Gospel values, and, occasionally, glimmers of an intense mysticism. This teaching was a first attempt to create a rationale for such a radical search for God and to formulate principles to govern the lifestyle of those who embraced it and to encourage them to continue. To struggle with contrary imaginations is normal, the elders said. It is a necessary part of the process of purification. Hold firm and trust in the Lord.

Monastic tradition took a step forward with Evagrius of Pontus. A well-educated man, he came to live in monastic Egypt after a much-needed conversion. His great achievement was to condense the wealth of wisdom that he found in the desert into systematic teaching. Much influenced by Origen, the great theologian from Alexandria, Evagrius described the monastic experience in terms of the exodus of ancient Israel from Egypt toward the Promised Land. Between departure from enslavement to the powers of darkness and arrival at the desired destination were forty years of wandering in

Garden work at Gethsemani.

Evagrius of Pontus
345–399

The bee house and hives.

the desert. This was the time of temptation. Just as the Chosen People had to do battle with a variety of hostile tribes that threatened their progress, so the monk, if he is to continue the spiritual journey, has to confront a host of contrary tendencies within himself. Monastic life is not a life of quiet passivity but an active and ongoing struggle with different forms of innate resistance to the call of God. Monastic life is spiritual warfare.

Beyond this practical wisdom, Evagrius was a profound teacher of contemplative prayer whose words still resonate today. He understood that the capacity to become absorbed in God was a consequence of the years of courageous struggle against one's inner demons. By resisting the attractions of the vices, the monk begins to experience the peace that comes when the heart is no longer divided against itself. He becomes single-hearted, integrated, and free from the tyranny of instinctual impulses. Thus he begins in some small way to experience the truth of Jesus' promise that the pure and single-hearted will see God.

DISCERNMENT

As the monk devotes his energies to living an authentic life he becomes aware that the principal danger to his vocation is not the world, which is constantly calling him back, nor the flesh, which has its own urgent priorities, nor even the varied temptations of the devil. The great enemy is self-will: the ego, wanting to maintain full control over his life and his environment, the cupidity that lacks a sensitivity to any need or desire but his own.

In its grossest form self-will is abhorrent to those around us and so it has to be disguised. Nobody likes to be called selfish. Because we like to think of ourselves as virtuous, vices rarely present themselves in their true colors. Major temptations will often present themselves under the semblance of a higher good—or as the avoidance of an undesired outcome. "You will not die," the serpent said to Eve, "but you will be like one of the gods." And so the greatest temptation faced by the inexperienced monk is to allow himself to be drawn away from the austere singularity of his ideal toward the alluring mirage of some alternative: "I would be better off as a preacher or a pastor or the father of a Christian family." When the monastic endeavor begins to gain pace, and the work of purification begins to bite, the great temptation is to terminate the process and to seek change.

It is in facing dilemmas like these that counsel is most important—and most resisted. Every newcomer needs to learn the art of spiritual discernment, to distinguish between what is real and life-giving from what is merely illusory and will ultimately lead nowhere. Discernment is learned by practice, and practice involves making many mistakes. The tradition of the desert was that the young monk needed to submit himself to the guidance of an experienced elder and to put aside any thought of remaining the master of his own life. He had to learn humility through the recognition and avowal of his own failures and limitations. It was the kindliness and humanity of these battle-scarred spiritual guides that communicated to the next generation the courage to continue the journey which they had begun.

Meanwhile a parallel channel of discernment was finding recognition. The monastic goal of freedom from the passions and from self-will remained the same. But, in the absence of charismatic guides, a disciplined life remained possible by following a recognized rule and living in harmony with others pursuing a similar ideal. In the West, the beginnings of the community or coenobitic style of monastic life owes much to the work of Saint John Cassian. Strongly influenced by Evagrius, he traveled around the Egyptian desert quizzing the most experienced elders for their views on the living of the monastic ideal. Their responses he transcribed and translated into Latin. These twenty-four *Conferences* provide a comprehensive overview of the spirituality that sustained the great monks of the Egyptian desert,

Saint John Cassian
360–435

now made available to those who would pursue the same ideals in colder climates. In addition to the *Conferences,* Cassian also composed twelve books of *Institutes,* which included not only systematic spiritual teaching but also practical regulations governing the life of a monastic community. These books served as inspiration and guide to later monastic rules, including the Rule of Saint Benedict, which became the guiding light of all monasticism in the West.

ORDER

Saint Benedict lived in tumultuous times. The Western Roman Empire had been shaken to its core when Alaric the Visigoth had sacked Rome in 410. In the century that followed, Italy was wracked by repeated invasions as well as natural disasters, disease, and famine. In the same period, the unity of the Church was fractured by many

The monastery is a school of the Lord's service where Christ is formed in the hearts of the brothers through the liturgy, the abbot's teaching and the fraternal way of life. *From the Order's Constitutions*

heretical movements. Benedict's vision of an alternative life was one in marked contrast to what he witnessed around him. He wished to create a monastery that would be an island of tranquility protected from the social and moral turmoil that surrounded it.

Benedict's monastic teaching is expressed through a rule, written for those who truly seek God and "are willing to serve in the army of Christ the true King." He proposed a strenuous life of good works undertaken in the context of a rule, an abbot, and a community, a life in which self-will would be progressively renounced and heartfelt desire for God liberated from its constraints. Benedict saw that the way to prepare for this gift of grace was to live daily life under the guidance of the Gospel. He drew from tradition the elements of a lifestyle that would allow monks to follow Christ in a way that was both radical and possible.

To live by the Gospel requires a person to have thoroughly assimilated what the gospels teach, and so Benedict made ample provision for the formation of his monks in scriptural doctrine and monastic tradition. There were readings during each Hour of the liturgy, especially at the nocturnal Office of Vigils. Meals were accompanied by reading, and an interval was left at the end of the day for the monks to come together to listen to reading before retiring. The final chapter of the Rule makes the point that monks who want to go beyond the bare minimum will immerse themselves in the teachings of the Old and New Testaments, the fathers of the Church, and monastic tradition.

Beyond this community reading, Benedict also prescribes that his monks spend several hours each day in personal reading (*lectio*

Lighting of the Advent wreath.

divina), its duration varying according to the season, the length of the liturgy, and the demands of manual work. It was only by constant contact with the Scriptures that the monk was able to maintain an intensely personal relationship with Jesus Christ that would serve as his motivation to live in accordance with the high ideals that his vocation entailed.

In contrast to the freewheeling existence of the desert monks, Benedict opted for a structured lifestyle. He understood that a regular and disciplined life gradually becomes second nature and so liberates the human spirit to turn more often to God. These moments of contact allow a personal relationship with Christ to flourish, which will color every activity and encounter of daily life. At first such a life seems hard and restrictive, but as the monk advances in union with God and allows himself to become accustomed to his chosen vocation, the monastic observances are experienced as life-giving and even delightful.

The skeleton around which the monastic day is formed is the regular celebration of the Liturgy of the Hours. Benedict termed this the *Opus Dei*, "the Work of God," because he deemed it to be the monk's principal task. The Hours of the Divine Office call a monk back to prayer from wherever else his other activities may have led

him. The Hours are like the rungs of a ladder by which he slowly ascends to God. "Nothing is to be given precedence over the Work of God," Benedict wrote, because he realized that the exercise of hearing God's word and responding to it throughout the day is a key component in learning to live mindfully under the loving gaze of God.

Saint Benedict was a practical man and he understood that few are able to spend the entire day in liturgical worship. And so he made provision for other activities that would together create a balanced lifestyle: time spent in sacred reading, time spent in work. There was to be an opportunity for all kinds of mutual service in the maintenance of a peaceful and fraternal environment. "Idleness is the enemy of the soul," he wrote, and he wanted his monks to avoid it by a harmonious variety of occupations that would equally benefit the doer and those on whose behalf the tasks were done. The traditional monastery was like a village containing within itself all kinds of necessary activity and, as a result, able to include persons of different temperaments or aptitudes.

Benedict was careful to establish a system of governance that would serve to maintain good order in the monastery and to assist the monks in reaching the goals they had pursued in embracing monastic life. The abbot was to have all authority in the community,

both spiritual and temporal, but other officials were appointed by him to take charge of particular areas of responsibility. By concentrating authority in a single office, Benedict aimed to ensure that priority would be given to the spiritual. "Above all, let him not overlook or undervalue the salvation of the souls committed to him; let him not expend more energy in taking care of passing earthly matters." Benedict sees the abbot as called to be an icon of Christ in the community, one who "knows that he has received the charge of taking care of weak souls rather than exercising a tyranny over those who are healthy." He is to imitate the example of the Good Shepherd, forming them by sound teaching and reinforcing in the community a climate of meaning sustained by the beliefs and values of the Gospel. In this way, under his guidance, the monastery will truly become "the household of God."

Each community of the Order and all the monks are dedicated to the Blessed Virgin Mary, Mother and Symbol of the Church in the order of faith, love and perfect union with Christ.
From the Order's Constitutions

MODERATION

The monks in the Egyptian desert expressed their fervor through individual lifestyles that were often extreme. Saint Benedict realized that a way of living designed to last a lifetime needs to be such that sufficient oil is left to keep the lamp burning to the end even of a long monastic career. And so he insisted that the abbot was to ensure that the monastic regime would be suitable both for the strong who desire a more fervent life and for the weak who may be intimidated if too much is asked of them. Moderation is not mediocrity. It is, rather, the fruit of an intelligent assessment of the capacities of each. He wrote, "Each has his own special gift from God: one this and another that." A monastery is not an army: there is room for diversity according to the nature and grace of each.

Moderation is akin to another of Benedict's values: reasonableness. It is not so much a question of watering down traditional observances to make life more comfortable for the monks. Taking up Benedict's frequent use of the image of running, it could be said that moderation is the fruit of a prudent judgment about the speed of progress most likely to be sustained until the end of the race. Monastic life lasts for decades; it is a marathon, not a sprint. The monastic athlete begins slowly, maintains a steady speed throughout life, and then picks up pace for a burst across the finishing line. This will not happen if he burns up all his energy in the early stages.

Stability is a prime Benedictine value and the object of one of the

monastic vows. The monk promises to persevere in monastic life until death. Monastic perseverance is not the result of a sturdy temperament or an inability to envisage alternatives. It comes about mainly through the gift of prudence and the grace of patience, concrete expressions of a living faith in God and of a serene hope in God's promises. The monk who has his gaze fixed on the ultimate goal of monastic life is able to endure many trials, seeing them as no more than slight momentary afflictions compared to the glory that lies ahead.

Patience, perseverance, and stability are the forces that shape the monastic environment and impart to it the characteristic note of peace. A monastery becomes a haven of peace not because of its location or its architecture but because it is home to men who desire to live in the presence of God and who make God the center of their daily lives. Monastic peace is a gift of God: it is not of human manufacture. It is, rather, the fruit of a life given entirely to seeking God, the ultimate source of concord and harmony.

Moderation prevails in a monastery because Benedict insisted that "the house of God be wisely administered by wise men." The result of such sage governance is that "nobody will be upset or saddened in the house of God." Ambition, suspicion, and excessive zeal are banished. Benedict enjoins on all his monks the duty of respecting and honoring one another, serving one another, defeating their self-will by giving precedence to the wishes of others, doing all in their power to make the monastery a paradise on earth, a communion of saints that already anticipates the coming of God's kingdom.

Monastic peace
is a gift of God:
it is not of human
manufacture.

HOSPITALITY

A life lived in accordance with the Rule of Saint Benedict is a life lived in the context of others. Coenobitic monasticism is not the cohabitation of solitaries but a real community where the brothers support one another by their cheerful presence, their work, their fraternal counsel, their forgiveness, and their prayer. The true follower of Saint Benedict develops a hospitable stance in daily life, a willingness to welcome not only friends but all comers, imitating the attitude of God who does not discriminate between persons, permitting the sweet rain of his favor to descend on all alike.

Saint Benedict sees this fraternal love as being manifested especially toward those who might otherwise be perceived as nuisances because of their weaknesses of body or of character. Concessions are to be made for the immature and the aged, and those who are seriously ill are to be given priority access to the goods and services of the community. "Care is to be taken of the sick before all else and above all else, since Christ is truly served in them. He himself said, 'I was sick and you visited me.'" Benedict encourages his monks to reach out beyond the borders of natural affection toward those who are in real need.

The same principle holds good in the welcome extended to strangers who present themselves at the monastery gate. It is not so much a matter of welcoming friends and benefactors or of providing a routine service of accommodation for travelers. It is an attitude of welcome extended to any who arrive under any circumstances. For Benedict, welcoming strangers warmly and humbly is a moment of

For Benedict, welcoming strangers warmly and humbly is a moment of encounter with Christ, hidden beneath an unfamiliar face but really present.

Tending the goats at the monastery of Mvanda in the Democratic Republic of Congo. Opposite: Monks of the monastery of Koutaba, Cameroon, at prayer in choir.

encounter with Christ, hidden beneath an unfamiliar face but really present. In a startling turn of phrase Benedict avers, "Christ is adored in them for it is he who is welcomed." The more unlikely this seems, the more Saint Benedict insists: "With all care and diligence a special welcome should be given to the poor and to travelers, since Christ is more surely welcomed in them. For the terror inspired by the rich is itself sufficient for them to be honored."

Saint Benedict's concern for the poor is evident in other texts. He wants the doorkeeper to have a room near the gate so that the poor are not kept waiting. He makes provision for the surplus clothing of the monastery to be made available to them. Above all, in a beautiful phrase, he asks the community to re-create the poor, to help them make a new beginning, to impart confidence where hope was none. The monastery wall may be intended to keep the world at a distance, but true Christian charity easily surmounts it. In centuries past when monks ventured into areas not yet evangelized they often undertook pastoral activities and cared for the sick so that, by its good works, the monastery became a force for evangelization.

The monastery following the path traced by Saint Benedict also shared its immaterial resources. Because *lectio divina* is such an important component of the monastic day, monks needed books and monasteries needed libraries. An ancient maxim read, "A monastery without a library is like a military camp without an armory." In their work of copying manuscripts for their own use, monks played an important role in the preservation of ancient civilization during the centuries in which learning was little prized in the outside world. During these

dark days of ignorance monks continued to read books; they copied books and wrote books. They established schools so that others also could read. The monasteries became important centers of culture, and their hallmark was, as a significant monastic scholar of our own times has expressed it, "the love of learning and the desire for God."

The contribution of the monks to the life of the Church was particularly evident in the area of liturgy. Because monks spend several hours each day in liturgical worship, they attain a high level of proficiency in the skills that enhance the celebration. This was particularly true in the matter of Gregorian chant. Even today, monasteries are places where the spirits of the Christian faithful are uplifted by the beauty and solemnity of the liturgy. This is another instance in which monastic life floods over its banks and is of benefit to a wider community.

AUTONOMY

In the centuries following Benedict, monastic life that followed the pattern prescribed in the Rule became a significant element in the Christian landscape. Monasteries owned large tracts of land, and their treasuries contained considerable cultural and material riches. Settlements grew up around the cloistral buildings, and the monastic precincts were transformed into a kind of village containing within itself all the arts and crafts necessary for a civilized life. The abbot was not only the leader of the monastic community; he had become the spiritual and temporal lord of all who lived in the shadow of the monastery. The villagers were dependent on the monastery not only for pastoral care but also for employment, medical services, education for their sons and, in times of natural disasters and famines, generous practical assistance.

External involvement and the absence of any effective form of supervision meant that there was a great deal of variation in the quality of monastic life followed in different monasteries. When men who were great saints and competent leaders took the helm, the monasteries flourished and attracted many high-caliber recruits. Spirituality and culture flourished. When lesser men were in charge the quality of monastic observance declined, beliefs and values were diluted, and the community became stagnant or dysfunctional.

From 628 when Pope Honorius I granted to Saint Columban's monastery of Bobbio a degree of autonomy, monasteries became effectively independent in a way that had much wider application than Benedict ever envisaged. While duly submitting themselves to the appropriate civil and ecclesiastical powers, the larger abbeys were self-governing, particularly in matters of internal discipline and observance and in the administration of their temporal domain. Because of their vast landholding, however, abbots became important people with a voice in both ecclesiastical and civil affairs; their monasteries became enmeshed in the complicated networks that passed for politics in that period. The result was an increasing encroachment of secular authorities in monastic affairs and a consequent decline in the necessary intensity of monastic living.

In the early ninth century, the first great institutional reform of Benedictine monasticism was initiated under Saint Benedict of Aniane. This second Benedict aimed to bring about some level of uniformity of practice among all the monasteries that professed to follow the Rule, since observance of it was often eclectic. To achieve this end, he persuaded the emperor to convoke a synod of abbots, some of whom were also zealous for reform. A group of abbots came together at Aachen between 816 and 817. As a means of affirming the spiritual character of monasticism and of improving the quality of liturgical worship, the Rule of Saint Benedict was established as the single

Saint Benedict of Aniane
750–821

Synod of Aachen
816–817

Racks of fruitcakes coming out of the oven.

rule to be observed in all the monasteries of the empire, and an effort was made to bring local customs into harmony. Compliance was to be ensured through the work of inspectors who were to visit all the monasteries of the region.

Concern for the excellence of liturgical services was at the heart of the reform associated with the abbey of Cluny and its dependent houses. For two centuries, under the guidance of five long-lived and holy abbots, it would exercise a powerful influence over the monastic world in Western Europe. Yet Cluny's temporal success eventually led to its spiritual decline. It began as a reformed monastery, but it became an empire, with its satellites spotted across much of the map of Europe and its wealth beyond estimation. It boasted the largest church in Christendom, and its elaborate ceremonial provided a benchmark for liturgical splendor. Cluny possessed artistic treasures of every kind, an extensive library, and a reputation for scholarship. The abbot of Cluny and the grand prior were personages to be reckoned with. Meanwhile, all this external involvement meant that attention had been diverted from the fundamental purposes for which monasteries exist: the humble search for union with God. As the range of activities increased, so did the motivations of those who entered. Those seeking a simple life began to look elsewhere.

Cluny
910

Fresh bread coming out of the oven.

Everything in the household of God should be appropriate to monastic life and avoid excess so that its very simplicity can be instructive for all.

From the Order's Constitutions

POVERTY

The eleventh-century reform movement often associated with the name of Pope Gregory VII spawned many different initiatives that attempted to breathe new life into the ancient institution of monasticism. Among them are some which have remained in vigor until the present. Often founded by charismatic leaders these reformed monasteries tried to put some bite back into monastic life by insisting on a stricter and more focused observance of the Rule. They often gave themselves the title "poor of Christ," expressing their commitment to live a life of poverty in imitation of Christ, often choosing to live apart from population centers, spending long hours in prayer, and supporting their simple lifestyle through manual labor.

One of those who experimented with a variety of monastic lifestyles was Robert of Molesme. The founder and reformer of many monasteries, Robert seems to have been a man who easily attracted both donations and recruits. The monastery of Molesme which he founded had some thirty-five dependent priories within twenty years of its foundation. It had, however, become the bustling center of an ever-expanding enterprise, even though Robert himself seems to have been in constant search of a purer expression of the monastic ideal.

After many such attempts, Robert set out with a group of his most fervent monks to establish not far from Dijon the New Monastery, later called Cîteaux. He remained abbot of the foundation for a little over a year and then returned to Molesme, where he lived until his death in 1111.

The foundation of the New Monastery in 1098 marks the beginning of what would become the Cistercian Order.

Communal anointing of the sick.

Pope Gregory VII
1073–1085

Saint Robert of Molesme
1028–1111

Cîteaux
1098

REFORM

Saint Alberic
1050–1108

Saint Stephen
1059–1134

Robert's successor as abbot of the New Monastery was the prior, Alberic, a solid monk who was described as "a lover of the brothers." The eight years of his tenure was a period of consolidation, with the formulation of the main principles of the reformed observance, the building and consecration of a stone church, and the securing of the monastery's future by obtaining official approbation from the Holy See.

At Alberic's death, his place was taken by Stephen, originally from Dorset in England, where he had been called Harding. Many scholars suspect that it was Stephen who was the driving force behind the reform in its early days as well as its champion through the quarter century in which he was both abbot of Cîteaux and the head of the rapidly expanding order.

After some fifteen years the New Monastery began to make foundations and not long after its twentieth anniversary was suffi-

Christmas celebration in the scriptorium, which is usually a quiet reading room.

ciently numerous to require the writing of constitutions and statutes to ensure that the principles of the reform continued to be implemented. Saint Stephen was not an empire builder; he was a firm believer in local autonomy. He did, however, recognize that total independence can lead to decline unless there are structures to safeguard the purity of observance. And so he wrote a constitution for the new Order. He titled his text *The Charter of Charity.*

Inevitably, the original structures Stephen put in place were subject to adaptation and fine-tuning as the Cistercian Order became larger, more international, and subject to a variety of local situations. Fundamentally, he wished to ensure that the austere lifestyle followed at Cîteaux would be fully adopted in every new monastery, but it was unanimity he sought rather than strict uniformity. To achieve this he made provision that every community, while remaining autonomous, was subject to the supervision of the abbot of the

Charter of Charity

1119

Silence is counted among the principal monastic values of the Order. It assures solitude for the monk in community. It fosters mindfulness of God and fraternal communion. It opens the mind to the inspirations of the Holy Spirit and favours attentiveness of heart and solitary prayer to God. *From the Order's Constitutions*

monastery from which it sprang. Thus he instituted a pyramid of filiation (the relationship of motherhouse to daughterhouse) that would avoid placing all responsibility in the hands of the abbot of Cîteaux. The ultimate authority belonged to the General Chapter, an annual meeting of all the abbots of the Order under the presidency of the abbot of Cîteaux. In this way, local communities retained their freedom of action but abbots would be held accountable for their decisions by their brother abbots. Essential to Stephen's thinking was the idea that each community would retain complete control over its own life and finances; there would be no taxes paid to the Order. There was, however, a strong insistence on mutual aid. Monasteries were encouraged to be generous in their support for communities experiencing financial or other difficulties. The most common response of the General Chapter to problems in communities was to send one or two abbots with special skills to see what could be done to improve the difficult situation. The bond uniting the communities was one of love and mutual support.

The earliest legislation of the Cistercian Order makes clear the priorities of the reform. The fundamental principle was a return to the purity of the Rule—abandoning the unnecessary accretions that had accumulated through the centuries. The founders sought to live an austere life of prayer and community supported by their own labor. This meant abandoning many sources of income that had sustained traditional monasteries: tithes, taxes, ecclesiastical stipends and offerings, and the ownership of the means of production such as ovens and mills.

Cistercian monasteries were not to use the indentured labor of serfs to run their farms. The monks themselves were to work on their land. Work was for them more than an economic necessity; it was integrated within their spirituality, an important component of the monastic day, keeping them in touch with their own bodies and with the land from which they drew their sustenance. For work that was such that it would regularly interrupt the daily rhythm of prayer and reading, the community was to rely principally on the services of laybrothers—religious under vows who formed part of the commu-nity and who lived a simple life of work, devotion, and service to the monastery.

Internally, the community's lifestyle was shaped by the principle of poverty. In matters of food and clothing the monks were to remain within the limits sanctioned by the Rule of Saint Benedict. Even the

Work was for them more than an economic necessity; it was integrated within their spirituality, an important component of the monastic day.

liturgy was subject to restriction. Gold and silver were banished, as were fine silken vestments. Everything was to be plain and simple, without ornamentation or display. When it came to building permanent monasteries to house the growing number of monks, the same radical simplicity prevailed. The remnants and ruins of some of the ancient buildings remain. Their evident harmony and proportion reflects the single-mindedness of those they sheltered, men who chose to live for God alone.

RENEWAL

The first generation of Cistercians, like many of their monastic contemporaries, was concerned chiefly with reform. Their successors in the second and third generations, building on this foundation, embarked on a program of renewal which combined traditional and new elements to generate a form of monastic life that was remarkably attractive to the men of those times. Within some sixty years of existence, there were more than 350 abbeys of monks attached to the Order. The geographical spread of these monasteries, west to east, was from Ireland to Hungary and Poland and, south to north, from Spain and Portugal to the countries of Scandinavia. We cannot be sure of exactly how many monks and laybrothers each monastery contained, but some of them had populations in the hundreds. Everywhere, it seems, monastic life was flourishing. In England between 1066 and 1154 the number of monks rose from about 850 to over 5,500, including 1,400 Cistercians. There may well have been in excess of 10,000 Cistercian monks in Europe around 1150. There were fewer nuns, but their number was also rising.

The reasons for this vast inflow of recruits are complex. Partly it was the result of the timeliness of the reform and its correspondence with the deeper aspirations of the young men of that epoch. More especially it was due to the considerable drawing power exercised by Saint Bernard, abbot of Clairvaux.

Leadership has recently been defined as "the communication of moral energy." It is something more than celebrity or charisma. It involves motivating people to change their thinking and to participate in some collective action that is larger than their own preoccupations or ambitions. And leadership is more than sparking an initial change in another's life. It involves maintaining the momentum in those who

Saint Bernard of Clairvaux
1090–1153

take up the challenge, without allowing their energies to be diverted or depleted, despite a variety of unexpected situations.

Bernard certainly possessed the quality of leadership. This gift did not consist only in the force of his personality or in his personal charm. He caught his fish with the hook of intellect. It was the loftiness of his teaching and the beauty of his language that won his listeners' attention. He was one of those people who are able to express clearly what others are thinking and feeling but are unable to put into words. Bernard expounded a vision of Christian life that inspired and motivated those who heard him. In particular, he pointed to the Cistercian monastery as the place in which all their highest aspirations could be nurtured and brought to fulfillment.

EXPERIENCE

Once these new recruits arrived in the monastery Bernard continued to guide them by sound monastic teaching. According to Saint Benedict's Rule, the abbot is to form his monks in monastic beliefs and values through regular teaching. Cistercian regulations in the twelfth century provided that the abbot should give a daily commentary on the Rule in chapter and also that he should give a more formal developed talk on the major liturgical solemnities. We have the written versions, or at least summaries, of about seven hundred of Bernard's talks, given over his nearly forty years as abbot. These had a wide diffusion not only in his own Order but throughout the monasteries of Western Europe.

Bernard did more than recycle the established truths of Christian faith proclaimed through many centuries by the fathers of the Church. He translated these truths into a contemporary language that reflected the attitudes of his time. He spoke about the mysteries of the faith not in themselves but in how they impact us. He was interested in our experience of grace, what the great truths of our religion feel like when they are accepted wholeheartedly and how they shape our everyday behavior. He had the ability to communicate his own enthusiasm by words that were pleasing to the ear as well as appealing to the mind. He spoke to his monks in an intimate, familial way; the tone of his addresses was warm, fraternal, and often humorous.

The twelfth century was one in which a keen interest in human subjectivity developed. It was the age of chivalry, the troubadours,

Fr. Matthew Kelty († 2011).

and popular love poetry. It has been suggested that it was around this time that the notion of the dignity of the individual began to be highlighted in the West. Spiritual teachers focused more sharply on the nature of the "inner life"—not in opposition to outward observance, but as its necessary concomitant and the determinant of its moral quality. It was not enough to engage in objective goodness; virtuous action had to spring from appropriate subjective dispositions. It was not enough to "do charity"; one had to "feel charity" as well. Moral progress was seen to consist more purely in the transformation of individual consciousness than in the amendment of outward behavior.

Even though Bernard was a passionate proponent of the reformed observance of Cîteaux, he realized that too much concentration on punctilious performance could lead to a delusional self-confidence that would be akin to pharisaism. The inner self could not be redeemed by outward actions. Only God's grace could accomplish that miracle. What the monastery aimed to do was to teach the monks how to be attuned to grace, and to do this they had to develop the skills of looking within, of returning to their hearts, of developing a consciousness of the work of the Holy Spirit in their souls.

For Bernard, the principal dynamism in the spiritual life was desire for God, innate in every human being but often covered over or subverted by distraction, selfishness, and multiple desires. The purpose of all monastic observance was to restrain these contrary forces and to allow each monk to discover within himself a deep attraction to spiritual reality and, at least, the beginnings of a profound love for God. For Bernard, the human being created to God's image and likeness was incomplete without God. He could not think of religion as an optional extra. A personal relationship with God was the necessary condition of human fulfillment. It was for this we were created and redeemed, and it is the perfection of this relationship that will constitute our happiness for all eternity.

Mowing in the préau.

For Bernard and other Cistercians, self-knowledge was the primary asceticism, and it was to inculcate this profound awareness of the self in relationship with God that the monastery existed. A typical Cistercian community of the period was seen as a school of self-knowledge. The prized virtue of humility was regarded not so much a matter of outward humiliation or lowly status. It was to be identified with a truthful attitude to self, to others, and to God. In a fully humble monk, ego and self-will disappear and his whole being becomes transparent. Even his outward appearance is transformed by the divinizing light that has taken possession of him. As this process continues, the monk is understood to be progressing toward a more complete humanity in which he will become more capable of reaching out beyond himself in self-forgetful love.

They saw the monastery as a school of love, where those whose lives were previously lived under the banner of self-love come to learn a higher mode of this essential human activity.

Saint Aelred of Rievaulx
1110–1167

LOVE

The twelfth century was an age of heightened affectivity and "love" was its keyword. Not surprisingly, the Cistercian thinkers made this concept their own, correcting popular notions with traditional New Testament teaching, grounding it in their own experience, and embellishing it with an elevated language that raised the idea of love above the cruder understandings that sometimes prevailed in the society around them. A good example of this was Saint Aelred's reworking of Cicero's treatise *On Friendship* into his own exposition, *On Spiritual Friendship*. Cistercian authors were highly responsive to ambient culture, but they reinterpreted it to align more fully with their own loftier ideals.

The Cistercians of the twelfth century aimed to create not only observant communities in which the Rule was kept punctiliously. They certainly wanted to achieve this, but only as a means to affective community, in which the brothers lived in an ambience of genuine charity. They saw the monastery as a school of love, where those whose lives were previously lived under the banner of self-love come to learn a higher mode of this essential human activity. In the chapter talks given by abbots of this period to their monks it is clear that love was not an abstract reality merely to be esteemed and celebrated. For them, it was a practical, everyday imperative. Living in community with persons dissimilar to themselves, monks had to learn and relearn the practical art of love. This meant not offending

others by roughness and insensitivity, treating them with courtesy, giving them respect, and, further, treating all their brothers with the honor that belongs to them as beloved children of God. It is from these behavioral choices that genuine affection, friendship, and love proceed. Bernard, Aelred, and Guerric of Igny spoke lyrically about love, but they were all convinced that to be sincere and lasting it had to begin with ordinary manifestations such as civility, self-control, thoughtfulness, kindliness, and a pleasant disposition. And for love to endure, it needed to be buttressed by much patience, tolerance, and thoughtfulness.

Because love is outgoing, it is not confined within the boundaries imposed by conscious identity or self-interest. Genuine love is necessarily unrestricted and unconditional, as is God's love for us. In ever-widening circles it reaches out to embrace, with the arms of concern, affection, and prayer, the whole of God's creation. It is within the context of this universal connectedness that the soul begins to experience some direct connectedness to the unseen God—the God who loves, calls, guides, helps, admonishes.

This profound attachment to God is purely spiritual, in the sense that it is the fruit of the Holy Spirit's interior action and also in the sense that it is not the fruit of any external action or initiative. Yet it overflows into human sensibility where it is experienced as devotion. For the medieval Cistercians, devotion was the deep feeling of the heart that accompanies a life dedicated to holiness and virtue and a will fixed with great intensity on God alone. It is not surprising that

Blessed Guerric of Igny
1075–1157

this sense was often associated with a personal attachment to Our Lady, the model of faith and humility. There was no trace of frothy sentimentality in this conception. Devotion was seen as the soft consequence of following with fervor the hard road that leads to God.

In liturgy, in *lectio divina*, and in the exercises of the common life, the monk is being continually admonished to "taste and see that the Lord is good." It is through this experience that, without any direct effort on his part, his love for God becomes more a matter of the whole heart and the whole mind. Prayer begins to invade his thoughts unbidden, and slowly the monk begins to move toward that unbroken attention to God that has been the ideal of monks in every generation.

CONTEMPLATION

There is a strong mystical current evident in the writings of the twelfth-century Cistercians. They taught that an enduring effort to live in conformity with the divine will brought a person to a point of clarity by which, from time to time, the opacity that clouds our relationship with God was dispersed, and a closer union with God was experienced. This conformity of will was achieved only after much struggle and, even then, imperfectly. It was seen to consist in bringing order into one's affectivity so that God was loved most and primarily and that everything else was loved—really and sincerely loved—as a consequence. Closeness to God makes us more like God. It necessarily enables us to see the goodness and loveableness of all around us and energizes us to act in accordance with that perception. When affectivity is thus brought into harmony then, when the mind and heart are disengaged from external distractions, there is a tendency for it to swing back naturally in the direction of God. This simple looking toward God is not triggered by any external event or even by a determined act of the will; it simply happens.

Sometimes this momentary sense of God's nearness lengthens itself so that for a time God seems as close as the objects of the material world—or even closer because the sense of God seems to penetrate even to the very core of being. This experience was described by Saint Bernard and others as receiving a "visitation" from the Word. Entirely the work of grace—untouched, as it were, by human hands—the visit of the Word brings the soul to an extraordinary

The spiritual character of the community is especially evident in the celebration of the liturgy. The liturgy strengthens and increases both the inner sense of the monastic vocation and communion among the brothers.

From the Order's Constitutions

state of alertness and aliveness. This changed awareness begins in the depths of the heart, enlightening the mind and intensifying the affective powers and sometimes overflowing into the emotions and bodily sensations. According to the oft-cited verse from the book of Revelation: "There was silence in heaven for half an hour."

This mystical encounter with God is at the heart of the monastic experience. It cannot be produced directly by any human means, but it is often a reflection of the unseen quality of a person's life. Ecstatic love is a matter of being absorbed into the one who is loved. It is a standing away from self—that is the root meaning of "ecstasy"—a radical form of self-forgetfulness. To the extent that preparation is possible, it can be anticipated through self-denial, through the gift of self to others, through service of the neighbor, through the blocking of self-will in obedience. Nearly all the elements of monastic observance, if embraced generously, serve the purpose of making the human heart more responsive to the interior

summons: "Behold the Bridegroom is coming. Go forth to meet him."

The image favored by the medieval Cistercians to describe the intimate mystical awareness that is the proper outcome of monastic life was spiritual marriage. The notion is not well understood or appreciated by our contemporaries. Far from being the solitary achievement of a spiritual athlete, contemplative union is a gift to the whole Church and through the Church to the world, tightening the bonds of love between the Creator and creation. When he interprets the Song of Songs so as to refer to the spiritual ascent, Saint Bernard makes it clear that what he writes applies both to the individual seeker and to the Church. Both are to be considered as drawn into union with the Word becoming, as he often writes, one spirit with him.

The contemplative life in its purity is a life lived in the heart of the Church, for the Church, so that all people may be saved and come to the knowledge of eternal truth. Although the experience

itself is solitary and personal, it is always an experience of solidarity and communion. This intense and hidden life is certainly not confined to those who live in monasteries, but it is the ultimate purpose of all monastic living. It is, as many popes have insisted, an unseen source of apostolic fruitfulness for all the Church's visible ministries.

RESILIENCE

The twelfth century was a high point of Cistercian history. There is, however, a universal law in human affairs: what goes up must come down. In the centuries following the death of Saint Bernard, Cistercian monasteries were subject to forces from within and without that constituted a grave threat to the survival of the Order. Recruitment was reduced due to demographic change and a different outlook on life. There were many newer and more exciting religious orders and the universities exerted a strong attraction. The profitability of basic agrarian economies was reduced; smaller communities faced financial difficulties while the more famous and well-established monasteries were often indecently wealthy. The imposition of secular abbots, with no interest beyond financial gain, led to a decline in observance. The Black Death carried off up to two-thirds of the monastic population. Schisms and wars made communication between monasteries impossible, and thus General Chapters and visitations became rarer. In England, Scandinavia, and elsewhere the rise of Protestantism meant the general suppression of monasteries. By 1600 few monasteries had more than twenty monks. In the 1780s the

> # Although the experience itself is solitary and personal, it is always an experience of solidarity and communion.

Catholic Habsburg Emperor Joseph II dissolved over seven hundred monasteries as "utterly and completely useless to their neighbors." In 1766 the Commission of Regulars in France closed 458 religious houses, and, following the French Revolution, all monasteries in territories under French control were closed. In the following century,

many European countries experienced waves of secularism, which
led to the suppression of monasteries. To many it seemed that monastic life would soon be extinct.

Meanwhile, the Order was divided within itself; monastic observance had declined, and there was much wrangling about details
such as the practice of abstaining from meat. There were intermittent
attempts at reform, but these were often frustrated by a lack of
consensus, by political divisions within the Order, or by interference
from secular or ecclesiastical authorities. In 1563 the Council of Trent
promulgated its decree on religious life, and the desire for the renewal
of religious life was in the air. Thirteen General Chapters were held in
the following century, with a view to implementing a program of
reform, but no agreement was ever reached. Reform initiatives

He understood clearly that the only way Cistercian life could survive in the climate of his times was to be single-minded in following the monastic ideals as these were presented in ancient monasticism.

Abbot de Rancé
1626–1700

Augustin de Lestrange
1754–1827

usually occurred at the local level, animated by a reforming abbot; sometimes clusters of abbeys formed to promote their ideals, and gradually the movement of Stricter Observance gained momentum. Monasticism was beginning to bounce back from the brink.

COURAGE

Armand-Jean Bouthillier de Rancé was a cultured and worldly cleric who had become the secular abbot of La Trappe at the age of eleven. After a series of events in his personal life triggered a crisis, he underwent a conversion and in 1663 entered the Cistercian novitiate to begin life as a monk. He understood clearly that the only way Cistercian life could survive in the climate of his times was to be single-minded in following the monastic ideals as these were presented in ancient monasticism. The austere life that he prescribed was a reaction both to the worldliness of his own previous existence and to the demoralizing effects of so many compromises in existing monastic observances. It was a way of life that directly challenged the ethos of the world around him.

As with all the French monasteries, La Trappe did not survive the revolution. In 1791, to escape persecution and to preserve the Trappist way of life, Augustin de Lestrange led a group of more than twenty monks to refuge at La Val Sainte in Switzerland and, when threatened there, took his group on an odyssey through various

Thomas Merton's hermitage.

countries until eventually he returned to La Trappe in 1815. And then the boom began. Within forty years there were twenty-three Trappist monasteries, and, by 1895, some three thousand monks in fifty-six monasteries belonged to this observance: stretching from Ireland and Spain to the Middle East, with houses in North America, China, Japan, South Africa, and Australia.

PENANCE

The Trappist regime, especially as codified by Lestrange, was more severe than anything in previous history, including Abbot de Rancé's reform. There was a strong emphasis on penance, perhaps animated by the notion of vicarious reparation, an important theme in the spirituality of the time. The monk was not so much atoning for his own sins but, in a spirit of solidarity, offering a counterbalance to the rejection of God and his Church so apparent on all sides. By his austere life, the monk was making silent intercession for a sinful world.

At La Trappe food was scarce and living conditions almost intolerable. A characteristic feature of Trappist austerity was strict and almost total silence, perhaps in reaction to the frivolity of the urbane conversations in the salons of Paris. In any case, because of their strict enclosure the monks knew almost nothing about what was going on in the world so that there was little about which they

could profitably converse. Silence was seen not only as a factor in ensuring a quiet ambience suitable for prayer but also as a means of avoiding the dissipation and detraction that can easily poison the atmosphere of enclosed communities. Inevitably, the silence observed by the monks was not as perfectly observed as their abbots may have wished, but it long remained a signature observance in all Trappist monasteries.

REUNION

The nineteenth century was one in which many monastic congregations spread their wings and flew to all corners of the globe. Whether it was to escape persecution or out of a fullness of life, monasticism broke away from the confines of European civilization and began to put down roots in localities with different climates and cultures. Meanwhile, the situation in Europe continued to be fraught with difficulties for monastic communities. The Cistercian Order was in a precarious position because it had effectively lost the organizational unity that had been its hallmark from the very beginning. Divided by both geography and observance, it was unable to present a united front to the challenges of its time. Eventually, with the strong encouragement of Pope Leo XIII, the three major Trappist congregations came together to form a single united Order with a single General Chapter serving its monasteries throughout the world. From this point, Cistercians of the Strict Observance continued to expand numerically and geographically through the first half of the twentieth century.

Second Vatican Council
1962–1965

ADAPTATION

The summons of the Second Vatican Council to updating and renewal opened up a period of profound self-questioning for all religious, not only concerning the external details of their daily life, but also regarding the spirituality by which they lived. Because many Trappist Cistercian communities had based their identity on the strictness of their regime, the time after the council was a difficult one, and many monks decided to seek their vocation elsewhere when the daily regimen began to be modified. Recruitment became more difficult, and changed eco-

nomic conditions meant that substantial modifications had to be introduced into the manual labor, long considered a typical component of Trappist life. As communities became less numerous they began to rely more on outside help for the continuance of some activities.

The time after the council has been, however, a time of grace. Because of the impact of the variety of local cultures and situations on the way monastic life was lived, the Order was led to accept that henceforth Cistercian observance would be marked by a certain pluralism. To protect the identity of the Order, the General Chapter of 1969 promulgated a *Statute on Unity and Pluralism,* which formulated the essential and signature observances that were to be followed everywhere. This text was to provide a reference point during the next twenty years while new constitutions were being formulated.

The translation of the liturgy into the vernacular made it more accessible to those who did not know Latin, and the reforms of Vatican II brought a wider and more fruitful selection of readings, especially in the Liturgy of the Hours. With the translation of monastic sources, the rich spirituality of the twelfth-century Cistercians began to be more widely available and was able to serve henceforth as the basis on which upcoming generations of monks were formed. At the same time, considerable efforts were invested in upgrading the quality of community life. Regulations were eased to make daily life less regimented and less institutional, with a lot more concern for the well-being of persons and their ongoing development. On a more universal scale, cooperation and collaboration between communities has contributed to a wider sense of communion and this is an ongoing source of encouragement and strength. Following the lead of the council, communities began to understand themselves in the context of the Church. This was expressed in a more generous hospitality that transcended confessional boundaries and by ecumenical and interreligious dialogue.

It is a fact that today communities in the Western world are generally much smaller than they used to be, and some are in precarious situations. Monastic work is less poetic and more businesslike. Monastic life has been divested of much of its mystery. This is a source of disappointment to many who hope to find in the monastery a life unchanged since the Middle Ages. But a monastery is not a museum. In every age monks have been obliged to fine-tune their lives to accord with the times in which they lived. It is a challenge and not a defeat.

Statute on
Unity and Pluralism
1969

Those periods in which monasticism flourished have been those in which monastic communities have most fully engaged with the reality of the world they inhabited. There is no fixed formula for a perfect monastery. The monastic charism continues to develop even as people and societies evolve from one period to the next. Meanwhile, although contemporary monasteries may not manifest the extraordinary brilliance of the twelfth-century Cistercians, mere size does not prevent our striving in an undramatic way to live the ordinary, obscure, and laborious life envisaged by the founders of Cîteaux and followed in different forms for more than nine centuries.

TRADITION

Tradition is more like a verb than a noun. It is not a static collection of material and behavioral artifacts that can be preserved indefinitely for the edification of future generations. Tradition is the act of handing on something precious to the next generation. What we do not always understand is that what is handed on is always modified in the very act of transmission. Bernard's brand of Cistercian monasticism was not identical to that of the three founders. Likewise, each generation translates what is received into its own idiom. Just as the outward forms of monasticism have changed over the centuries, so they will continue to change in our time and in the future. What is unchanging is the lifelong search for God in a simple communal life of prayer, reading, and work.

The values inherent in monastic life are relatively constant. Nevertheless, we have seen that at different times and in different situations particular values have become important as the flag-carriers of the monastic impulse: flight from the world among the Desert Fathers, good order for Saint Benedict, love and contemplation among the first Cistercians, resilience in times of social upheaval, courage when reform has been called for, creative fidelity in an era of renewal and rapid social change. All the values about which we have spoken are important, but their individual relevance to a particular situation varies from one place to the next. The different ways of observing the Rule of Saint Benedict that we find in different monastic congregations and even in different communities of the same Order derive from their use of different formulas for blending the

various values. Some groups are more solitary, some more communitarian. Some are more urbane, others more rustic. And the proportions can change with time.

Who knows what the future holds for Cistercian life? Already the center of gravity has moved away from Europe and from the large institutional monasteries that have been its mainstay in centuries past. This may represent a call to return to a simpler lifestyle that does not demand large buildings and complex economies, a relatively uncomplicated life in which there is ample leisure for reading, reflection, and prayer. The future will probably demand a fuller fraternal life less contaminated by rampant individualism as well as a purposeful and disciplined lifestyle that provides clear directions to newcomers. The same goal our forebears embraced is that toward which we travel now and it will remain so in the future. For our successors, however, the scenery by the roadside will, almost certainly, be different.

The founding concept of the Cistercian Order was *caritas*, charity. As the Cistercian grace is incarnated and inculturated in many different regions, perhaps by persons as yet unborn, it is above all the gift of communion in love that will provide the key to monasticism's future flourishing. The Cistercian way of life is a great treasure by virtue of its disciplined way of life and its rich spiritual heritage. The greatest privilege of modern-day monks is the opportunity to enrich what they have received and through their own dedication and generosity to pass it on enhanced to those who will come after us, so that in all things God may be glorified.

The future will probably demand a fuller fraternal life less contaminated by rampant individualism as well as a purposeful and disciplined lifestyle that provides clear directions to newcomers.

FROM THE OLD WORLD TO THE NEW

By Clyde F. Crews

FIRST GLIMPSES — GETHSEMANI ABBEY TODAY

THE ABBEY OF GETHSEMANI stands before the visitor today as a quiet, sacred space where "silence is spoken." As American places go, it is truly old—over 160 years of life in this same location. It is a place of deep traditions, yet it lives and thrives with an openness to the Spirit and service to the Church urged by the Second Vatican Council.

Its guesthouse welcomes over four thousand visitors a year. Some of its monks are involved in scholarly activities like congresses on medieval studies and in initiatives like Cistercian Publications and *Cistercian Studies Quarterly*. They have worked together with such groups as the International Thomas Merton Society and the Lay Contemplatives of Gethsemani. Men of many talents and backgrounds make up the lively community. Published poets and writers, artists and photographers, technical and business experts are all to be found in their midst.

Abbey visitors will probably not be surprised to find at Gethsemani today the architectural treasures of the Abbey Church and Skakel Chapel, or a well-stocked book and gift shop, or the accessibility

of a monk for spiritual conversation. But they may not be expecting expansive acres of strikingly handsome Kentucky landscape: forests and fields, lakes and streams. And it may surprise them to know that the monks have access to phones and newspapers or that computers are not strangers to the place.

To appreciate the Abbey of Gethsemani more fully, it may well be useful for the wayfarer to pause for two brief inquiries: One would be an examination of the rich history of this sacred place. The other would be the exploration of the inner depths of a Cistercian monk's life in our own time. To these twin purposes, the following pages are devoted.

THE HISTORY OF GETHSEMANI ABBEY: AN INTRODUCTION

Pilgrimage is a journey undertaken in the light of a story. —Paul Elie

The narrative that follows brings before us—in brief telling—a small group in history on a special kind of Christian pilgrimage: that of the monastic life. More particularly, what follow are glimpses into the life and times of the historic Abbey of Our Lady of Gethsemani. Nestled in the heart of the famed "Kentucky Catholic Holy Land," this storied monastery continues its pilgrimage of faith, contemplation, and service

in an age that is often cynical and disillusioned. This journey is driven by the Gospel story in all of its simplicity and complexity.

The saga of these monks—very human people hoping to become both more human and more holy—can offer a healing message to a much wider world community. Their famed tradition of hospitality welcomes thousands of day visitors to the abbey each year. It also invites us to listen to their long history and, in listening, learn more about the possibilities of life's sometimes radiant, often challenging, journey.

To tell the story of this oldest Cistercian abbey in the United States, we first reach back to situate its founding in the occasionally surprising context of the history of Catholicism in America, especially in its first major inland development, that of the Kentucky frontier.

I. OUT OF THE PAST

The American Catholic Context

When the American Republic came to birth in 1776, the nation was not particularly religious, from an institutional point of view. Historians estimate that somewhat less than 20 percent of the population held membership in any particular congregation. The numbers would rise dramatically throughout the nineteenth century—in large part due to immigration—and peak at about 60 percent in the 1950s. That figure has held relatively stable, even into recent times.

Handwritten account of the founding of Gethsemani by Dom Eutropius Proust (left). The abbey cemetery (right).

In those days when America was so young, Catholic citizens, about twenty-five thousand in number and constituting about 1 percent of the total population, formed a distinctive minority on the national scene. And where were most of these believers in the ancient faith to be found? The answer will surprise many today. It was not in the Northeast. Neither New York City nor Boston had a single Catholic parish church at the time of the American Revolution. Nor was it around the Great Lakes, a region that didn't see substantial urban development until a later generation. Nor was it along the West Coast, which wasn't included in the Union until the decade before the Civil War.

In fact, until at least the 1830s, most Catholics lived in the South, below the Mason-Dixon Line. Their place of greatest concentration had been Maryland, the only original "Catholic colony" that had been settled in 1634. Baltimore, in fact, would be named the see city of the first United States Catholic diocese in 1789. All Catholics in the entire country would be under the leadership of the bishop of Baltimore until the nineteenth century was well under way.

The Kentucky Equation

As soon as the revolution ended, many Maryland Catholics began to turn their eyes to new territories in the emerging western country. It was not so much a question of religious freedom as the fact that they sought better farmlands and the opportunities afforded by an expansive new nation. And so they began their migrations to Kentucky, then still part of Virginia, a territory that historian Alistair Cooke would call "the first American West."

Here, in the region around the little settlement of Bardstown, they began to come in "leagues" or groups, beginning in 1785. And here, within the next twenty and more years, they would establish a network of parish communities, first called by the name of the nearest creek, rather than by any saint's name. And unlike the East and West Coasts where Jesuit or Franciscan priests established the early churches, the frontier Kentucky Catholic congregations often had to lean on the laity for leadership.

To be sure, they had the occasional brief services of a priest, but it was not until the arrival in 1805 of Fr. Stephen Badin and Fr. Charles Nerinckx that they experienced the stability of regular, ongoing, lasting clerical ministry. Both were refugees from the French Revolution, and Badin had the honor of being the first priest ordained in the United States. Also in 1805, a vanguard of Dominican priests arrived in Kentucky, making their first American foundation in the area of Springfield, about fifteen miles east of Bardstown.

In 1808, Pope Pius VII established Baltimore as an archdiocese and created four additional dioceses for the United States: New York, Boston, Philadelphia, and Bardstown, the latter being the first inland see of the new nation. To Bardstown, the Holy See assigned as bishop Benedict Joseph Flaget, yet another exile turned out of France by revolution. This former professor was forty-five years of age and none too eager to assume his new task. Who could blame him? The area he was charged to administer was larger than France itself, and over forty other dioceses have since been carved from his vast jurisdiction. In fact, it was over three years after his appointment, in the summer of 1811, that Flaget arrived in his Kentucky diocese.

Clockwise from far left:

The monastery of Géronde, Switzerland.
Bell tower at the Abbey of Novy Dvur, Czech Republic.
Sixteenth-century library at the Abbey of Citeaux, France.
Refectory at the Abbey of La Trappe, France.
A sister of the monastery of Butende, Uganda.

Br. Patrick Hart (left).
Br. Norbert Meier (right).

With diocesan status came an amazing burst of creative energies, all centered in the Kentucky Holy Land within about a twenty-five-mile radius of Bardstown. In the years between 1811 and 1822, the following appeared on this frontier landscape, many of them firsts in the American West: a seminary (St. Thomas); a cathedral (St. Joseph's); three religious communities of women (Sisters of Loretto, Sisters of Charity of Nazareth, and the Dominican Sisters); three colleges for young men; and several academies for young women. A little over a decade later, the first Catholic newspaper in the West was begun at Bardstown.

With diocesan status came an amazing burst of creative energies, all centered in the Kentucky Holy Land within about a twenty-five-mile radius of Bardstown.

It was a dazzling record, and one that was surpassed at the time only by the mother archdiocese of Baltimore. Soon this cradle of American Catholicism was exporting many of its religious leaders around the country. Eight of Flaget's priests were to become bishops themselves. This was all the more remarkable in that this hardy, creative group of Catholics—lay, clerical, and religious—continued to be a small minority in the larger and growing population of the Kentucky Commonwealth. In 1841, because of its especially rapid growth, Louisville, the city aside the Ohio River about forty miles north of Bardstown, became the new seat of the diocese.

A Monastic Overture

While Catholicism was aborning in the new Republic and on its
burgeoning frontier, France, "eldest daughter of the Church," was
torn with turmoil and revolution, more often than not hostile to
Catholic interests. In particular, the monastic orders came under
scrutiny and repression. France had been a homeland to a vast
number of abbeys, including Cîteaux and Clairvaux, that had been

foundational in the twelfth century to the Cistercian Order, a reform wing of the ancient Benedictine tradition. In the seventeenth century, a further reform infused such monasteries as La Grande Trappe and La Val Sainte and yielded yet another expression of the Cistercian tradition. As monks from so many of these abbeys found themselves ousted from their religious homes, they naturally turned to other countries in Europe for shelter and safety. A few hardy souls even thought of turning to the far-flung land of America.

With Kentucky Catholicism still in the midst of its early formative intensity, it was not surprising that it should be a welcoming host to monastic refugees. And so it was in the autumn of 1805 that some twenty Cistercian monks reached the landing in Louisville, on their way to seeking a monastic home. This group, ousted from their monastery of La Val Sainte by forces of the French Revolution, had already, in 1803, attempted to find a home near Conewago, Pennsylvania. But their leader, Dom Urban Guillet (1764–1817), was a restless man and

moved repeatedly. In Kentucky, he met a kindly welcome from Fr. Badin and his coreligionists. In fact, for a fleeting moment, both Frs. Badin and Nerinckx flirted with the idea of joining the order.

For only a brief time Urban and his monks settled on a farm near Holy Cross, the earliest of the Kentucky parishes. Founded in 1785 (the same year New York City got its first Catholic church), Holy Cross continues today as a lively parish. In the cemetery that surrounds the parish church there, a large memorial stands for eight Trappists who died in this region during their Kentucky sojourn.

In 1807, just two years after settling around Holy Cross, Urban moved his community again, though still within Kentucky. This time he took them about thirty miles away to Casey Creek, near St. Bernard parish. On the farm there, the monks sought to enhance their livelihood by the production of clocks, watches, and silverware. But a fire at the monastery and floods nearby were all the justification a man like Urban needed to move on. And so in April 1809, he and his band were off to Florissant, Missouri. Shortly thereafter, it was to Cahokia, Illinois. In 1814, when conditions improved in France, they left America behind and returned to their native soil. Thus did American and Kentucky Catholics get a brief, though peripatetic, preview of a monastic community.

In Kentucky, it would be nearly thirty years before another group of monks came their way. Many would still remember the wandering community of La Val Sainte with appreciation and happy memory. They would be ready to extend again their best Southern hospitality.

II. THE FIRST FIFTY YEARS
STORM AND STRESS: 1848–1898

Getting There

By the early 1840s, despite some unsettled times, conditions had at least temporarily stabilized in France, and some of its monasteries were again flourishing. A case in point was the Abbey of Melleray near Nantes. There, Abbot Maxime was confronted with a monastery filled far beyond its means. He also feared that the national political complexities could erupt again at any time and cause disruption. Accordingly, he sought to form a branch or "daughterhouse" foundation.

America beckoned. And the Diocese of Bardstown–Louisville had, as we have seen, significant connections to the Church of France. Not the least of these was the venerable old Frenchman Flaget, still bishop at Louisville. In 1847, Fr. Paulinus, the prior at Melleray, made a preliminary visitation to Kentucky and arranged a purchase of land about twelve miles south of Bardstown. There, the next year, the delegation of monks from Melleray would make their adventurous way.

Chosen to lead the colony was Fr. Eutropius Proust, thirty-nine years of age, described in later years by Thomas Merton as a "thin, wiry, intense little man . . . full of ideals." In his charge were forty-three other members of the Melleray community. On the dreary morning of October 26, 1848, dressed in secular clothing, they departed their monastic home on foot for the first seventeen miles. They traveled through France by steamboat and the new technological marvel of the train, but not without having their fifteen thousand pounds of baggage lost for a worrisome time. They took ship on the *Brunswick* from Le Havre on November 2. One of their number, the seventy-year-old Italian Fr. Benezet, died in transit and was buried at sea. The forty-three survivors made landfall at New Orleans on December 11. From there, they boarded the steamboat *Martha Washington* to Louisville via the Mississippi and Ohio Rivers.

Delayed briefly at the canal just below the city, Fr. Eutropius

disembarked and made a preliminary visit to the residence of Bishop Flaget next to the Louisville Cathedral. In a moving scene, the aged and weeping prelate received his visitors with the biblical words: "Blessed be those who come in the name of the Lord." By evening, the *Martha Washington* had docked at the city's downtown wharf. The prudent Eutropius later recalled that in the darkness at the landing, his little flock was "surrounded by street-walkers and loungers." To protect them and their baggage, he gathered wood along the riverbank, built a large fire, and had the monks encircle it. All of them accepted Flaget's hospitality for a time of rest in cathedral schoolrooms.

Continuing their journey, the forty-three monks made their way

In exchange for the steady assistance of the neighbors, Fr. Eutropius promised that the monks would offer free schooling to the nearby children.

south to Bardstown, there visiting the Jesuit fathers who staffed St. Joseph's College. At last, on the rainy morning of December 21, 1848, they completed their last few miles, reaching the tract of land that they would make their new monastic home.

There, in Nelson County, they found the fifteen hundred acres that Fr. Paulinus had arranged to purchase from the Sisters of Loretto for $5,000. The tract stood about four miles west of Fr. Urban's

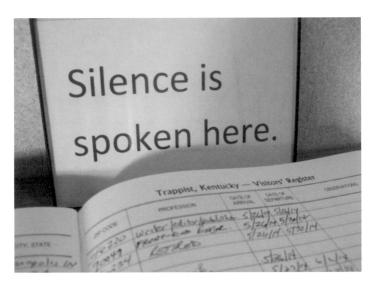

previous cloister near Holy Cross. The sisters, under the leadership of Sr. Teresa Grundy, had opened a school on these same lands in 1818. The school, named Gethsemani by Fr. Nerinckx, had lasted for thirty years, being closed shortly before the monks arrived.

Settling In

Some small cabins and buildings remained in place, but the monks immediately began clearing the land and planning for new construction. In exchange for the steady assistance of the neighbors, Fr. Eutropius promised that the monks would offer free schooling to the nearby children. But first, before anything else, the community would begin their daily round of prayer and chanting that has continued without interruption to this day.

Father Eutropius was taken ill shortly after the arrival but recovered sufficiently to make a fund-raising tour of Europe in 1849. He met with Pope Pius IX during this tour, and as a result of his petition, Gethsemani in 1851 was officially granted the status of an abbey. An abbey, of course, had to have an abbot and—to no one's surprise—Fr. Eutropius was elected to the post by the community in May 1851. The following October, in splendid ceremonies, he was duly blessed at the cathedral in Bardstown.

The new abbot had a herculean task in organizing, financing, and constructing this first abbey of the American South. In 1851, a free school for boys was begun, partially fulfilling the promise to neighbors. The following year, William Keely, the architect who had designed the American Gothic cathedral in Louisville, was also engaged to design the monastery building and the abbey church. On March 25, 1853, the feast of the Annunciation, the cornerstone of the abbey was placed. The building's design was influenced by the architecture of the motherhouse at Melleray. A careful accounting at the time reported that over three million bricks were used in construction.

Wearied by all his responsibilities, Abbot Eutropius resigned his abbacy in 1859, returning to Melleray. The population of his abbey at that time stood at sixty-five men, most of the new recruits who had been added having been from Irish and German parentage.

Advancement and Austerity

The second abbot of Gethsemani, chosen in January 1860, was Benedict Berger, one of the original settlers of 1848. His father had served in Napoleon's army, and there was something of a military austerity in Benedict's life and leadership. Forty years of age at the time of his election, Benedict would rule the community for nearly thirty years with a heavy hand. In *Waters of Siloe,* Merton describes Berger as having a "Napoleonic chin" and "steely eyes." And he says very tellingly of the rigid superior:

It must have required a very special kind of heroism to live through these twenty-nine years of very hard labor and real poverty, under an abbot whose deliberate policy was to insult and humiliate his monks at every turn.

(*Waters of Siloe*, p. 134)

Berger's early tenure coincided with the years of the Civil War. A legend relates the abbot's clever handling of Confederate guerrilla fighter John Hunt Morgan. More documentably certain are accounts of Dom Benedict's friendly relationship with a Union colonel that resulted in the abbey's gentle treatment in a hostile time. One very dramatic encounter occurred just after the war's conclusion. The abbey had engaged a Cincinnati plastering firm to complete work on the new monastery building. The abbey archives relate an anonymous threat from a self-proclaimed guerrilla sent to the abbot that read as follows:

Fr. Benedict: We understand that you have employed a Yanky [sic] to do your plastering. I would not like to put you to any trouble, but nobody from that side of the river can work out here. So be warned and avoid trouble.

In the event, the abbot relieved the Ohio company of its labors and employed a Louisville firm instead.

In the postwar years, the very presence of Gethsemani on the fringe of America's Gilded Age continued to fascinate the public.

Front view of Thomas Merton's hermitage (above). Hermitage interior (below, right). Thomas Merton and the Dalai Lama (lower left).

National publications and especially the newspapers in Louisville sent reporters every few years to write long accounts of their visits to the abbey. These were usually warily appreciative, though some disparaged the life and the men who led it. The widely known author James Lane Allen wrote *The White Cowl*, historical fiction with a Gethsemani setting. Kentucky governors began to make occasional visits, and their first ladies were even invited by way of exception into the cloister for reception ceremonies. The newspapers duly took note. Already here were legendary stories to report about some of the monks and their pre-monastic lives—true tales of a former Texas cowboy and of a European opera baritone. And, truth to tell, a genuine noble, the Baron de Hodiamont de Neau, was laid to rest in the monks' cemetery. He had been one of Dom Urban's pioneer monks who came to Kentucky in 1805. He later left the community, went into business, made a fortune, and in old age came back to board at the abbey until his death.

One of the notable men of this era who aspired to be a monk of Gethsemani was one Ira Dutton who entered the abbey in 1884. He was a Yankee originally from Vermont and had served the Union cause in the Civil War as a soldier from Wisconsin. Given the name Brother Joseph at the abbey, he stayed only a year and left without taking vows. But he went on to join the famous Fr. Damien in working

among the lepers of Molokai. Dutton died in Honolulu in 1931 at the age of eighty-eight, still known to one and all as "Brother Joseph."

During Benedict's tenure, the abbey changed in many appreciable ways. He saw to the completion of the monastery building and the spacious Gothic-style church, both solemnly dedicated in November 1866. In that same year he established a sisterhood, the Third Order of St. Francis, and provided for them a school to educate young girls. This was known as the Mount Olivet Female Primary School. But nearly from the beginning, stormy issues surrounded the venture. There were divisive quarrels about leadership within the sisters' own community, and this in turn caused division between Gethsemani's abbot and Louisville's contentious Bishop William George McCloskey. In 1873, Gethsemani summarily closed the school and with it any more ventures in female education.

Meanwhile, the school initiated for boys as early as 1851 had continued to grow and was incorporated by the Kentucky General Assembly in 1868. By 1881 it acquired the status and name of Gethsemani College. The school served mainly young boys in their teens, both day students and boarders. The student body never exceeded two hundred in number. Rules were strict and only Catholics were admitted. Christmas vacations were excluded because, according to the 1891 catalog:

Experience has taught that the breaking up of the first session by the Christmas Holidays has a most injurious influence, intellectually, morally and physically.

The catalog intoned additionally:

Spitting on the floors . . . or veranda and all other vulgar habits unbecoming young gentlemen [are] prohibited.

To guard against . . . danger to morals, incident to the reading of frivolous or bad literature, no newspapers, pamphlets, periodicals etc., are allowed, except those approved by the Rev. Fr. Abbot.

Elements in the monastery considered that entirely too much energy was expended by the community in staffing the institution. Additionally, it pulled the monks away from any time for contemplation and plunged them deeper into educational ministry that was not at the heart of their vocation.

Then, in the mid-1890s, rumors, to which many of the monks gave credence, began to swirl around the headmaster, Darnley Beaufort. Yet the abbot failed to act. At last, financial and moral charges were pressed against Beaufort in Nelson County Court, and he was sentenced in April 1896. The man who caused the trouble had been rooted out, but the damage was done. When the entire school was destroyed by fire in March 1912, fortunately, no one suffered major injury. Nor were many of the monks saddened by the loss. Gethsemani College was immediately closed forever. A statue of Saint Joseph facing the main monastery crowns the hill today where the school once stood.

Br. Luke playing the Létourneau organ (left). Inside the bell tower (right).

The Gloomy Time

In fact, it would be conditions at the college that brought about the crisis that ended the tenure of Gethsemani's third abbot. This was Dom Edward Chaix-Bourbon, who held the top office from 1890 to 1895. He was sociable, wrote Merton, but therein lay his main problem. He was not a good judge of character. So aggrieved were the members of the community in the wake of all this turmoil that they confronted Dom Edward directly. They drew up a list of seven grievances and asked their abbot bluntly: "Have you not been weighed in the balance and found wanting?" They wanted his resignation, and after some vacillation on his part, they got it.

Merton called this the "gloomiest period of Gethsemani's history." The monastery population stood at sixty-six, two-thirds of them lay-brothers, the rest being priests or "choir religious." But to have an American enter the abbey and remain there was still a rarity. The question became: is Gethsemani truly viable as an American abbey?

For a time even the Melleray motherhouse appeared unresponsive to cries for help from Kentucky. But at last the abbot general dispatched one of his Alsatian monks to take charge and restore harmony and stability. Gethsemani was about to be transformed utterly, because of the man who was dispatched. He was Fr. Edmund Obrecht, and he reached Gethsemani on March 25, 1898. This stalwart cleric from Alsace was elected by unanimous vote of the community to be their fourth abbot on October 11, 1898. The abbey in Nelson County would never be the same again.

III. A GROWING AMERICAN CLOISTER: 1898–1948

The Monastic Wonder

Dom Edmund Obrecht was, by all accounts, a force of nature, a monastic wonder. He was a man fashioned of the most diverse elements. He was a contemplative who crossed the Atlantic Ocean, by his own accounting, 161 times—and that in a steamship era. As a young man, he enlisted in the French army in the Franco-Prussian War. He traveled around the world as an emissary of the Trappist

Palm Sunday procession (right).

Order. He spoke several languages but demanded that his own monks, still heavily French by background, speak English—on the few occasions that they then spoke at all.

Dom Edmund had a wall built around the abbey to ensure monastic privacy, and yet it was he who initiated regular retreats for laymen at Gethsemani starting in 1921. In that same year, he shut down "The Bowery," the nickname that emerged for a set of rooms in the abbey that had long been set aside for penitent priests sent by their bishops from across the nation. Abbot Obrecht saw to it that the

abbey church obtained stained-glass windows. One of these, known as "The Milk Window" caused a small controversy. Based on a legend that resulted in several iconic portrayals in northern Europe in the late fifteenth century, the window showed the Blessed Virgin Mary holding the Christ child and at the same time bestowing a stream of motherly breast milk upon Saint Bernard of Clairvaux. This "lactation" would symbolize the gifts of wisdom and eloquence upon the monastic saint. According to notes in the series intriguingly titled *Gethsemani Speaks* in the abbey archives, the intrepid abbot was angered by the critics and "made a few highly flavored comments on this modern hypocritical attitude toward things that were sanctioned by heaven and the saints."

During the Obrecht years, numbers in the community rose, with an increasing number of American citizens appearing at the gatehouse. Just before America entered the First World War, the community held eighty monks. And still the French influence clung to the sensibilities of

Dom Edmund ordered the bells to be rung and a great *Te Deum* to be sung. But one wonders if his chronicler had even heard the names of President Wilson and General Pershing.

many a professed member. When the great day of Armistice arrived on November 11, 1918, the now-unknown keeper of the monastery annals wrote in the ledger words that had a distinctly Gallic point of view:

> The Armistice was signed on November 11, the Feast of St. Martin
> . . . spreading through the whole world the glorious victory of France
> and Allies due to the help of Almighty God, to the military genius of
> Marshall Foch and sagacity and patriotism of Premier Clemenceau.

Dom Edmund ordered the bells to be rung and a great *Te Deum* to be sung. But one wonders if his chronicler had even heard the names of President Wilson and General Pershing.

On visits to Lisieux in France, Dom Edmund established a deep friendship with the religious sisters of the then recently canonized Saint Thérèse, the Little Flower. Through his auspices, a special relationship was established between the French Carmel and Gethsemani, with many of the Kentucky monks enamored of Saint Thérèse's famed

Work scenes from the 1950s: (clockwise from upper left) refectory service, pipe soldering, tobacco farming, on the tractor, herding the dairy cows.

"Little Way" of spirituality by the sanctification of the ordinary.

From his travels, Abbot Obrecht brought back an amazing array of canes, photos, helmets, books, chalices, and all manner of cultural objects that he displayed in a specially developed museum. Through his eager desire to garner a great library for the monastery, he arranged for the donation of Milwaukee's Monsignor Leonard Batz's extraordinary library of thousands of books to be brought to Gethsemani. Some of these rare items, along with Obrecht's extensive collection of manuscripts and rare books, have now been put on permanent loan to the Institute of Cistercian Studies at Western Michigan University.

We get a small glimpse of the sometimes lordly Dom Edmund in his travels from a memoir kept by one of his monks as reported in *Gethsemani Speaks*. In 1926, the monk was the traveling companion to his abbot and met him in the center of swirling pedestrian traffic at Grand Central Terminal in New York City:

> *I bowed to kiss his ring. "Yes. Now take a blessing!" [said the abbot].*
> *I wondered how—in the rush hour at a big railroad station. . . .*
> *"Go down on your knees," [said the abbot]. . . . I did so whilst*
> *pagan, Christian and Jew looked on, asking one another if that person*
> *perhaps be the pope.*

The Monks' Daily Life

For the average choir monk of these years, the typical prayer day consisted of Mass and the Divine Office chanted in Latin throughout the day. Worship began at about two o'clock in the morning with the chanting of Vigils, Lauds, and Prime and concluded with evening Compline with its powerfully evocative singing of the *Salve Regina* in honor of the Virgin Mary. In this era, a number of previously private devotions were added in for community use as well.

For most of the community, the laybrothers in particular, work in the farm fields or craft shops provided the balance of the day. The diet was somewhat spartan, certainly vegetarian. Silence was strictly observed in most circumstances, with an elaborate sign language developed for necessary communication. Monks rarely traveled outside the monastery and wrote and received letters only at specified times of the year. In a weekly Chapter of Faults, they publicly proclaimed their violations of the Rule or perhaps listened while one of their brothers "proclaimed" them and announced their fault for them.

Celebration and Valedictory

The entire community of eighty-one monastics took part wholeheartedly in the great triple jubilee of 1924, which celebrated the seventy-fifth anniversary of the founding of the abbey, the fiftieth year since Dom Edmund's ordination as priest, and the twenty-fifth year of his rule as abbot. The great doors were swung open for visitors, impressive liturgy was celebrated, silence was relaxed for the community, and a great banquet was prepared for all. Heading the list of renowned visitors was one of Dom Edmund's closest friends, Dennis Cardinal Dougherty, archbishop of Philadelphia. His Eminence arrived with all the mighty pomp then afforded such ermine-clad prelates. He had earlier traveled from Philadelphia to Louisville's Seventh Street Station in a specially reserved railway car and had a similar accommodation on the train from Louisville to Gethsemani.

Abbot Obrecht continued as a "troubleshooter" for the Order, making both American and international visitations until nearly the time of his death on January 4, 1935. In a private diary kept by one of the monks, we learn that the entire community was summoned to their leader's deathbed. The old abbot passed away peacefully and without any struggle. The man who headed what was once thought to be an obscure abbey in Kentucky received a significant obituary in the *New York Times* the next morning.

An Experienced New Leader

The primary reason the abbey continued to run so smoothly during Dom Edmund's extensive travels is not difficult to discover. He trusted completely in the prior he undoubtedly was grooming as his successor. Fr. Frederic Dunne was the first American to attain the title of abbot at Gethsemani. He had entered religious life in 1894, served a term as head of Gethsemani College and was named prior in 1901. No sooner was he elected and installed as abbot in February 1935 than the abbey was struck by a ferocious attack of influenza that

The books used in choir (right) were printed, hand-sewn, and bound by the monks.

saw the death of eight monks within a few weeks. Louisville's Bishop John A. Floersh arranged for two Alexian nursing brothers to come to the abbey to attend the sick during the health emergency.

Dom Frederic was specially blessed with unusually talented men who enhanced the life of the community. Among these were two authors whom the abbot encouraged in their literary careers. One was Fr. Raymond Flanagan, who died in 1990, the author of such best sellers as *The Man Who Got Even with God* (1941) and *God Goes to Murderer's Row* (1951). The other was Fr. Louis, Thomas Merton, who will be

discussed below. Also among the young talent were to be found two architectural experts, Brothers Clement Dorsey and Giles Naughton.

Dom Frederic enhanced the intellectual life of his abbey not only through urging his writers onward. He also increased library privileges among some of the monks and improved educational curricula for student monks. Under the new superior's watch, indoor plumbing, telephones, and electric lights came onto the monastery grounds. Also in these years, numbers began to make their steep rise: 68 men in 1935; 82 in 1936; 126 in 1941.

*Scenes from the Welcome Center,
Gift Shop, and the reception desk
at the Retreat House.*

Rumors of War

Even though the monks of those years did not regularly get to read the papers or hear radio broadcasts, they were aware of the deepening world crisis. The official chronicler of 1941 wrote in the big bound journal:

> *We come to one of the saddest years in the world's annals, almost a premonition of the end of all. All the world, practically, is at war, and to make confusion doubly confounded, our own country was dragged in by a dastardly and treacherous perpetration on the part of Japan December 7, 1941. . . . Our Reverend Father whilst making the announcement, dwelt on the spirit of charity that should continue to be the bond of union within our monastic enclosure.*

And in 1945, he recorded:

> *Victory bells: August 14, the Vigil of Mary's Assumption. . . . The most eventful and frightful year in the world's history hitherto. Allies recaptured Philippines, brought Germany and Japan to their knees.*

In this section of the journal, the writer has pasted in a small notation, apparently at a later date, that Gethsemani's Brother Matthew (Rupert McGunigle), who had entered the monastery after the war, had been aboard one of the planes in the mission that dropped the atomic bomb on Nagasaki on August 8, 1945.

Branching Out

By early 1943, crowding at Gethsemani had become so intense that very serious consideration was given to the opening of a branch or daughterhouse. A vote was taken in Chapter on April 14, 1943, and by a margin of thirty-eight to four, the affirmatives triumphed. Although various sites were considered, including California and the Florida Everglades, the decision was made for the Honey Creek Farm near Conyers, Georgia, about thirty miles from Atlanta. Cost of the land was $45,000. Because of the impossibility of communicating with the Trappist authorities in Europe during wartime conditions, the abbot instead sought and received permission from the papal apostolic delegate in Washington. On March 19, 1944, Dom Frederic presented to his community the list he had drawn up of twenty

Simply professed monk receives the black scapular in Chapter (above). Recessional Procession on the Solemnity of the Assumption (right).

The monastery of Shuili, Taiwan.

monks who would shortly leave Gethsemani and make the new Abbey of the Holy Ghost their home. Two days later, the feast of Saint Benedict, they boarded a night train to Atlanta and were off on their mission.

On July 7, 1947, Dom Frederic dispatched thirty-four more of his monks to a second daughterhouse, that of Our Lady of the Holy Trinity in the Ogden Valley of Utah. This time the price tag was $100,000 for 1,800 acres, and the Parke farm was purchased although no buildings as yet stood there. Temporary housing was quickly provided by bringing in old army barracks and eventually metal Quonset huts.

Dom Frederic Dunne was traveling by train to make a visit to the monks at Conyers on August 4, 1948. Just as the train pulled into the Knoxville station, the abbot was stricken with a fatal heart attack. In Kentucky, in Georgia, and in Utah, the many monks who had begun monastic life at Gethsemani were suddenly shocked and grieved. Yet another era was ending for the abbey that was that very year observing its one hundredth anniversary of foundation.

Preparing the altar for a Solemnity.

IV. RENEWAL AND REFORM.
MID-CENTURY TO NEW CENTURY

An Intensity of Expansion

In its sixth abbot, Dom James Fox, Gethsemani found not only a
spiritual leader, but a business genius as well. With a background
in studies at the Harvard School of Business before entering the
monastery, Dom James was keenly attuned to the need for establish-
ing his large monastic estate on a firm financial footing. He was
responsible, after all, for 165 monks. And in the very year of his
election, 1948, 70 novices showed up, many of them veterans of the
recent Second World War. The monastery population topped out at
279 in the mid-1950s. Gethsemani had become the largest Trappist
monastery in the world.

It was imperative to make even more new foundations. And so in November 1949, Our Lady of Mepkin was established in Moncks Corner, South Carolina, on old plantation grounds donated by Henry and Clare Boothe Luce of *Time* and *Life* magazine fame. In 1951, a fourth branch was established at Our Lady of Genesee in upstate New York. Our Lady of New Clairvaux followed at Vina in northern California in 1955. Finally, a sixth house would be formed at La Dehesa near Santiago in Chile in 1966.

In Kentucky, too, intense expansion was the order of the day. With a small core of professionally competent monks around him, Dom James founded Gethsemani Farms as a business entity that

In addition to his studies in spirituality, he would also write on a wide range of subjects, including civil rights, nuclear weapons, war and peace, ecumenism, and Eastern religions.

would come to specialize in mail-order distribution of such products as cheese, fruitcakes and fudge. The farm capacity was expanded and modernized; the dairy herd improved; lakes and a water tower were built. These last two features are still evident on today's landscape at Gethsemani. The monastery was set now on a firm foundation indeed, though some monks complained that the historic grounds resounded a bit too much with business and industry.

Merton

One such critic was Thomas Merton, the author, who had arrived as a postulant in December 1941. At Dom Frederic's insistence, he continued his writing career, beginning with some poetry and pious biographies. But in October 1948, his autobiography, *The Seven Storey Mountain*, was published and became an unexpected literary sensation. It would spend months on best-seller lists and make the young monk an American household name—at least in many households. He was likened to the "American Saint Augustine" in some quarters. In the postwar confusion, his saga of a young man who struggled for meaning found ready and sympathetic readers. Even though in later years Merton would consider this early effort too "smug" of a book, it had cast its spell and had helped to cause some of the rush to enter the abbey.

Merton would produce over fifty books and several hundred articles. In addition to his studies in spirituality, he would also write on a wide range of subjects, including civil rights, nuclear weapons, war and peace, ecumenism, and Eastern religions. In 1965, Dom James gave Merton permission to move to a hermitage on the abbey grounds. His life was full of insights and energies, both intellectual and spiritual. He was also a man of great complexity as many of the biographies eventually written about him show.

On December 10, 1968, Merton was in Bangkok, Thailand, at a conference on monasticism. During a recess, he was accidentally electrocuted by touching a fan with faulty wiring. His body was flown back to Gethsemani for burial. In a front-page obituary, the *New York Times* spoke of the Kentucky monk as "a writer of singular grace about the City of God and an essayist of penetrating insight on the City of Man."

Many commentators take special note of an experience Merton

Clockwise: a boxed wheel of cheese, cheese racks in the curing room, decorating fruitcakes, fudge production, packaging line, bread day in the bakery.

*By constantly
cultivating
mindfulness of God,
the brothers extend
the Work of God
throughout
the whole day.*

From the Order's
Constitutions

had in downtown Louisville during a medical visit to the city on
March 18, 1958. They tend to see a shift in his concerns and topics to
more extensive and expansive subjects after this revelatory moment.
Echoing his themes of hidden hope and wholeness in the human condition, Merton wrote:

> *In Louisville, on the corner of Fourth and Walnut [now Muhammad
> Ali Blvd.] . . . I was suddenly overcome with the realization that I
> loved all those people, that they were mine and I was theirs, that we
> could not be alien to one another, even though we were total strang-
> ers. . . . There is no way of convincing people that they are walking
> around shining like the sun.*

And yet, in many ways, Merton spent the rest of his days trying to convince people of just that fact. Since his death, his reputation has continued to grow. Many of his books not only remain in print but have been translated into dozens of languages. A steady stream of books and studies about the man continues to flow from presses. He left the bulk of his literary estate to the Thomas Merton Center at Bellarmine University in Louisville. In 2008, the City of Louisville officially posted the name "Thomas Merton Square" at the old intersection of Fourth and Walnut Streets.

Conciliar Influences

Merton's influence was felt indirectly at the Second Vatican Council, especially in the areas of ecumenism and peace issues. He was a close friend and in frequent contact with a nearby Kentucky neighbor, Mother Mary Luke Tobin of the Sisters of Loretto, the only American Catholic woman to have an official role at the council. His correspondence with other council figures was significant, as was his friendship with his former Columbia University professor, Daniel C. Walsh, who had moved to Kentucky in these years to teach at the monastery. Dr. Jack Ford, a lay philosophy professor at Bellarmine and a lifelong friend to the abbey, came to teach courses on the Gethsemani grounds. Meanwhile, more monks were dispatched to Rome for advanced study.

Some trends in the Cistercian Order were already moving in directions of change after the Second World War. And then the Second Vatican Council (1962–1965) unleashed new energies and thinking across the Catholic spectrum, including life at Gethsemani. The two categories of choir religious and laybrothers were ended. Dramatically, on Holy Saturday 1965, the laybrothers changed their brown vesture for the same white habits worn by choir religious. Now all were to be simply Cistercian monks. Also in 1965 a new monastery library was opened. In 1968, the traditional sign language was dropped from general usage. Silence continued to be revered but was not as rigorously maintained. Correspondence became a more regular occurrence for all members of the community, and the Chapter of Faults was discontinued.

Additionally, very visible change became evident in liturgy and the extensive renovation of the abbey church. Chant was now in English. Architecturally, gone were the Gothic arches. Gone were

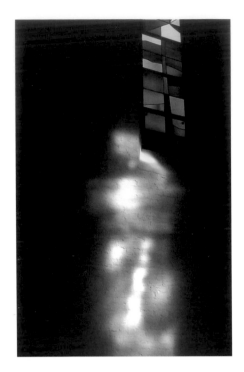

the old stained-glass windows. Gone were the devotional statues. In their place there emerged, from the design conceptions of architect William Schickel, a worship space that focused on simplicity and a chaste solemnity. Now, bare white brick walls and the original timber roof beams framed a soaring sacred space where eucharistic celebration and Divine Office would be paramount.

In 1967, Dom James signaled his wish to resign after some twenty years at the helm. He retired to a hermitage on a nearby property owned by the abbey where he lived for a considerable time. He died on Good Friday in 1987, at the age of ninety-one. Today his body rests beside that of his former confessor, Fr. Louis—Thomas Merton—in the abbey cemetery.

His successor, the seventh abbot, was Fr. Flavian Burns, who would hold the post until 1973. Most notably, he is said, in the words of Dianne Aprile in her history of the abbey, to have "quieted down" the monastery after the high intensity of the Dom James years. One of his first acts was to close the old gift shop. Deeply influenced by the Second Vatican Council, he sought to develop more communal involvement and a more democratic approach to community. He frequently urged in Chapter that a monk best enhances the community by attending to God's own special summons in his life. He arranged for every monk to have a private room rather than a mere cubicle. And when he resigned in 1973, he also retired to a hermitage on the monastery grounds, although he often was called forth to serve in leadership roles at other Cistercian houses.

Constancy and Change

In the year that the old Kentucky abbey was marking its 125th anniversary, it had once again to choose an abbot. The lot on this occasion fell to the Canadian-born, Rome-educated Timothy Kelly. He would hold the abbatial position for twenty-seven years, until 2000, and later would serve at the Order's generalate in Rome. Dianne Aprile described this eighth Gethsemani leader as "Energetic. Trusting. Modest. Democratic. Accessible. Sympathetic. A good listener. An instinctual leader."

Even a casual visitor to the abbey in these years would have noticed changes. The monastic population had diminished. Women were admitted for retreats, and the guesthouse itself underwent a striking renovation. Agriculture was becoming less a staple of the

*We sing songs seven times a day,
for ourselves and for the world.
We've been doing it since we got
here. We got here late in the after-
noon of December 21st, 1848.
The next day they began, December
22nd, and it has never stopped.
Every day, seven times a day, day
by day, week by week, year by
year, 'til the end. In a wild, sordid,
noisy, violent world, we sing. We
sing ancient songs rich in history,
graced by God, for our healing and
for the healing of the world.*

Fr. Matthew Kelty

monastery's livelihood. And the abbey was more visibly involved in using its resources to serve the poor of the neighboring region. Gethsemani helped to establish Habitat for Humanity in the area.

The ecumenical and interfaith profile remained high as well. About a quarter of all retreatants who regularly fill up the guesthouse are not Catholic in faith. In 1996 the abbey was host to "The Gethsemani Encounter," a gathering of Buddhist and Christian monks and nuns. The fourteenth Dalai Lama, who years before had befriended Merton, was among the participants. He thus joined the ranks of other world-famous religious figures who had visited the abbey, including Rabbi Abraham Heschel, philosopher Jacques Maritain, and Jesuit scholar Fr. Karl Rahner.

Some monks became particularly well known even beyond the monastery walls. Among these was Br. Lavrans Nielsen, the artist, who entered Gethsemani in 1957. Among his more visible marks are the icons and banners still to be seen at the abbey. Fr. Chrysogonus Waddell, who was professed in 1955, was an outstanding musicologist. He became particularly known for his extensive scholarship in the field of medieval studies, his most important works being editions of early Cistercian sources. He died in 2008. Fr. Matthew Kelty, writer and raconteur, was a man of endless wit and sage spirituality who delivered regular conferences to visitors. He was chaplain in the guesthouse for many years. Professed in 1962, he died in 2011.

The New Century Dawns

In the millennial year of 2000, the community of Gethsemani elected Fr. Damien Thompson as its ninth abbot. He was a former Maryknoll priest and a man of wide experience. He was succeeded in 2008 by Fr. Elias Dietz who was called back to Gethsemani from his work at the order's headquarters in Rome by the election of April 29, 2008.

Through it all, the bedrock constancies have remained. As the new century advances, the forty or so monks of Gethsemani maintain

their rhythm of life: prayer and work, contemplation and service, liturgy and chant. They enact and embody what Pope Francis recently urged of a cloistered community in October 2013:

> *Have great humanity, a humanity like that of Mother Church. . . . Be human. . . . Understand all aspects of life. . . . Be able to understand human problems. . . . Know how to forgive and to pray to the Lord for others.*

Such is the monastic journey in its search for God. The world continues to find fascination in it all and beats a path to the monastery door. The ancient Gospel story is ever new. The pilgrimage continues.

The organisation of the monastery is directed to bringing the monks into close union with Christ, since it is only through the experience of personal love for the Lord Jesus that the specific gifts of the Cistercian vocation can

flower. Only if the brothers prefer nothing whatever to Christ will they be happy to persevere in a life that is ordinary, obscure and laborious. And may he lead them all together into eternal life. From the Order's Constitutions

Monks Road is published by the monks of the Abbey of Gethsemani, Trappist, Kentucky.
It was designed and produced by James McDonald and Hans Teensma of the Impress Group
in Northampton, Massachusetts, in collaboration with a committee of five monks of the
abbey: Luke Armour, Gaëtan Blanchette, Elias Dietz, Lawrence Morey, and Paul Quenon.
It was printed using vegetable-based inks in four-color process with a spot varnish on
Creator Silk Text, a paper approved by the Forestry Stewardship Council, and contains at
least 10% post-consumer waste. It was printed, Smyth sewn, and bound by The Studley
Press, Dalton, Massachusetts. The typeface is Stickley, a humanist, old-style-based font
designed by Michael Stickley in 2009. The monks are the principal photographers of
Monks Road. Additional photographs on pages 17, 18, 40, 41, 98, 99, and 136 are by Thomas
Georgeon, ocso, La Trappe, France; 109 (right) and 144 by James McDonald; 2–3, 62, 97,
and 148–149 by Hans Teensma. The front cover photograph is by James McDonald.

ABBEY OF GETHSEMANI
3642 Monks Road, Trappist, Kentucky 40051
Telephone 502-549-3117
www.monks.org

Printed in the United States of America
First Printing, March 2015

ISBN 978-1-4951-4403-5